TABLE OF CONTENTS

CHAPTER 1

INTRODUCTION

Much has been written about the need to establish the rule of law in failing or failed states. Additionally, much has been written regarding counterinsurgency theory in light of the recent wars in Iraq and Afghanistan. Notwithstanding the large contributions made by scholars and practitioners in these areas, little has been written regarding a particular area in which these fields intersect. Scholars addressing this intersection primarily do so in the context of nation-building or post-conflict reconstruction. In other words, they focus their attention on the civilian justice institutions; namely, establishing and maintaining the civilian law enforcement, judicial, and corrections systems. Government civilian and military practitioners do the same and, unsurprisingly, this focus manifests in their doctrine.

Nevertheless, when security forces conduct counterinsurgency operations they are by their presence within the state, action against the insurgents, and interactions with the indigenous population impacting the rule of law within that state. Thus, it becomes apparent that security forces should consider whether or not adhering to the rule of law while conducting counterinsurgency operations is beneficial to defeating the insurgency. If following the rule of law is beneficial, it then follows that security forces should consider what factors assist or prevent them from conducting operations in accordance with rule of law principles. Scholars have yet to directly address these issues and, given the rich body of literature in both counterinsurgency and the rule of law, the lack of attention is unfortunate. I attempt stimulate the discussion with this thesis.

This thesis in comprised of five chapters. I present in chapter 1 a brief recitation of the counterinsurgency and rule of law concepts that I explore in more detail later. I also frame the research problem and explain its scope. I conduct a detailed review of the counterinsurgency and rule of law literature in chapter 2. I also introduce the causal framework that I later employ to analyze possible causal influences that prevent or hinder security forces from conducting operations in accordance with rule of law principles. Chapter 3 briefly explains that this thesis is a theoretic undertaking and that my methodology is comprised of a detailed review of counterinsurgency and rule of law theory.

I present my analysis in chapter 4 in three parts. First, I examine the current U.S. Army counterinsurgency rule of law framework and conclude that it is less suitable for use in counterinsurgency than the rule of law framework appearing elsewhere in U.S. Army doctrine. Second, I analyze counterinsurgency and rule of law theory and conclude that security forces that conduct operations in accordance with the rule of law are more likely to succeed at counterinsurgency. Third, I identify and examine several hidden or counterintuitive causal factors that assist or prevent security forces from following the rule of law during counterinsurgency.

I conclude in chapter 5 by making recommendations to modify current U.S. Army counterinsurgency and rule of law doctrine. I also identify areas where further research and consideration would be beneficial.

Background

In conventional war, military action is generally the principal way to achieve a political goal and politics as an instrument of war becomes secondary to armed battle between opponents. However, the nature of insurgency is political. This is an important distinction, because it leads security forces to place the indigenous population at the forefront of their concern. Both insurgent and counterinsurgent conduct operations to win the population's support or, at least, keep them submissive. These operations are essentially political in nature with politics an active instrument of the operations.

As might be expected, this is not an easy task. States with advantages in material, resources, population, territory, and economic power often find themselves at a disadvantage in small wars when the comparative strength of the opponents is not measured by these criteria. Operations become more difficult when a state's objective is to obtain political concessions or lack of resolve on the part of the enemy rather than the defeat of his armed forces.

As a result, scholars and practitioners have devised two counterinsurgency theories that address these factors. One is enemy-centric theory, which focuses on opposing the insurgents with violence by annihilating the popular base of insurgency, isolating the population from the insurgents, or selectively eradicating the insurgents and their leaders. The other is population-centric theory, which focuses on protecting the population and gaining their support. Though security forces may combine both approaches in various degrees, the U.S. Army's doctrine and practice favors population-centric theory. Thus, I focus predominately on population-centric theory throughout this thesis.

Counterinsurgency scholars contend that both the insurgent and counterinsurgent have two ways in which to compete for the support of the indigenous population. First, they can wield coercive power through the use of force. But, force has the potential to strengthen or weaken an insurgency; therefore, security forces must wield force only as an extension of credible coercive power. Second, insurgents and counterinsurgency compete for support of the population by fostering perceptions of legitimacy. This requires security forces to practice rectitude and employ force discriminately to intervene successfully in an insurgency.

Similarly, rule of law theorists insist that the rule of law is essential to the success of any intervention in a failed or fragile state. Yet, there is significant divergence regarding its meaning. Some theorists advocate a rule of law focused on rules and procedures rather than the substantive content of laws. As expected, others insist that the rule of law requires substantive commitments, although there is must disagreement over the type and extent of these commitments, e.g., should the rule of law protect basic human rights or do more such as promote democracy. Still others advocate for a synergistic approach that emphasizes the importance of reforming toward particular goals and not simply building rule of law institutions.

Notwithstanding the variance in rule of law theory, there is popular agreement regarding several basic tenets that together describe the rule of law. These tenets are thoroughly addressed in some U.S. Army doctrine, but somewhat incongruent in Army Field Manual (FM) 3-24.

Statement of the Problem

Counterinsurgency literature and U.S. Army doctrine favor a population-centric approach to counterinsurgency, of which the primary objective is to foster effective governance by a legitimate host nation government. This approach further prescribes that adherence to the rule of law is a major factor in assessing a government's legitimacy. I examine the theoretical basis of counterinsurgency and the rule of law, to determine if following the rule of law assists security forces in defeating armed insurgency. In other words, it is possible that practitioners assume that adhering to the rule of law supports counterinsurgency efforts; however, a close examination of the theoretical basis for this conclusion is warranted.

Moreover, if following the rule of law assists security forces in defeating armed insurgency, it follows intuitively that foreign and host nation security forces conducting counterinsurgency operations would conduct operations in accordance with the rule of law in order to enhance government legitimacy. Yet, the literature implies that several hidden causal factors act to influence security forces to conduct operations that that both support and conflict with rule of law principles. The areas of incongruity reduce government legitimacy and hinder counterinsurgency efforts. I describe these factors and categorize them by causal logic, e.g., institutional, structural, ideational, and psychological.

Research Questions

Does following the rule of law assist security forces in defeating an armed insurgency? Secondary Questions that support the answer to the primary question are the following:

1. How does insurgency and counterinsurgency differ from conventional war?

2. What are the theories of counterinsurgency and how do they assist in understanding insurgency?

3. What are the theories of the rule of law?

4. What is the relationship between counterinsurgency and the rule of law?

If following the rule of law assists security forces in defeating an armed insurgency, what factors assist or prevent security forces from conducting operations in accordance with rule of law principles? Are their novel and useful ways of identifying and describing these factors?

Limitations

This is a theoretical study of insurgency and the rule of law. I present only the aspects of insurgency, counterinsurgency, and the rule of law relevant to understanding why security forces conduct operations in accordance or discordance with the rule of law. I focus on the political nature of insurgency in order to afterward explain the relevance of the rule of law to counterinsurgency operations. I describe the two preeminent counterinsurgency theories, population-centric and enemy-centric, to illustrate that current U.S. doctrine and practice favors the population-centric theory. I identify and describe the pertinent aspects of the competing rule of law theories in order to discuss a rule of law framework applicable for use by security forces conducting counterinsurgency operations. I further limit the review of doctrine to current U.S. Army doctrine, particularly that concerning the rule of law, counterinsurgency, and stability operations.

Delimitations

Several topics of interest pertinent to the subject of counterinsurgency and the rule of law fall outside the scope of this study. As explained more fully in chapter 2, I discuss enemy-centric counterinsurgency and counterterrorism only for the purpose of illustrating that U.S. Army doctrine and practice favors population-centric theory. I do not examine the relative merits of population-centric and enemy-centric counterinsurgency theory, nor do I engage in a review of the less prominent counterinsurgency theories. Although I explore and describe the relationship between counterinsurgency and counterterrorism, I limit my analysis to counterinsurgency. I acknowledge that the analysis may be relevant to other military operations.

Additionally, I frame the rule of law discussion by reviewing the minimalist, substantive, and synergistic approaches to the rule of law. However, I do not address the merits of these competing theories other than to identify rule of law principles relevant to counterinsurgency.

Lastly, I identify and explore factors that assist or hinder security forces from following the rule of law and I acknowledge that there may be numerous relevant factors. However, I limit my examination to only those factors that I consider hidden or counterintuitive.

Significance of Thesis

The significance of counterinsurgency and the rule of law is apparent from the attention paid to them in scholarly publications and military doctrine. Further these areas are particularly significant given the recent protracted wars in Iraq and Afghanistan, in which these concepts, theories, and practices were widely employed. This thesis is significant because it address a gap in the current literature regarding this subject matter. Specifically, much has been written about counterinsurgency and the rule of law. Yet, little have been written directly examining the theoretical basis for whether following the rule of law actually assists security forces in conducting counterinsurgency and how this may or may not be so. Moreover, if doing so does provide assistance, military

7

commanders and political decision makers would benefit from understanding what causal influences assist or prevent security forces from following the rule of law. This is particularly important given my focus on the hidden and counterintuitive causal factors, which would otherwise go unnoticed or underappreciated.

CHAPTER 2

LITERATURE REVIEW

The broad and expanding literature on insurgency and the rule of law is much too large to survey thoroughly here, and so I present only the aspects relevant to understanding why security forces conduct operations in accordance or discordance with the rule of law. First, I focus on the political nature of insurgency in order to later explain the relevance of the rule of law to counterinsurgency operations. Second, I contrast the two preeminent counterinsurgency theories, population-centric and enemy-centric, to illustrate that current U.S. doctrine and practice favors the population-centric theory. Third, I describe how the population-centric counterinsurgency objective of protecting and gaining the support of the local populace is attained through two mechanisms: the use of the security forces' credible power to coerce and their ability to foster perceptions of legitimate governance. Fourth, I identify and describe the pertinent aspects of the competing rule of law theories in order to identify a rule of law framework applicable for use by security forces conducting counterinsurgency operations.

I provide an incrementally narrowing examination of the insurgency literature. This approach serves two purposes. First, it focuses on the relationship between counterinsurgency and the rule of law to allow us to explore in chapter 4 whether security forces benefit from following rule of law principles. Second, it allows causal factors to emerge from the literature, which have yet to be comprehensively identified or examined. These factors assist or prevent security forces to conduct operations in accordance with the rule of law. I identify and analyze these causal factors in chapter 4 to illustrate that hidden or counterintuitive factors influence security forces in conducting

9

counterinsurgency operations. Lastly, I conclude this chapter by describing the framework that I utilize in chapter 4 to identify and analyze these causal factors.

The Political Nature of Insurgency

Although there is no universally accepted definition of insurgency, there is enough agreement in the literature to offer a popular definition. Thus, I propose the definition formulated by Brad O'Neill that insurgency is the struggle between a non-ruling group and the ruling authorities in which the non-ruling group consciously uses political resources and violence to destroy, reformulate, or sustain the basis of legitimacy of one or more aspects of politics (O'Neill 2005, 15).[1] Importantly, insurgents seek to replace an existing order with one that conforms to their political, economic, ideological, or religious vision (Gompert and Gordon 2008, 23), and use political resources and instruments of violence against the ruling authorities to accomplish their goals. For example, insurgent political activity includes such things as the dissemination of propaganda, protest demonstrations, recruiting personnel, training and infiltrating agents into official institutions, appeals to external powers, financiers, creating support groups, providing services to the populace, and devising strategies (O'Neill 2005, 32).

However, identifying these insurgent political activities does not provide a comprehensive understanding of the political nature of insurgency. Thus, we must contrast insurgency and conventional warfare. Though scholars agree that all wars are

---

[1]Military doctrine defines insurgency as an organized, protracted politico-military struggle designed to weaken the control and legitimacy of an established government, occupying power, or other political authority while increasing insurgent control (FM 3-24 2006, 1-2).

fought for political purposes, they distinguish insurgency from conventional war (Galula 1964). In conventional war, military action is generally the principal way to achieve the political goal, but politics as an instrument of war tends to take a back seat and emerges again, as an instrument, when the fighting ends (Galula 1964, 8). Conversely, the very nature of insurgency is political. Writing specifically in regards to revolutionary wars, Galula finds that the object is the population itself with operations designed to win over or to keep the population submissive being essentially of a political nature (Galula 1964, 9). In other words, politics is an active instrument of the operations.

Asymmetry, another significant difference, is a prominent area of existing insurgency research concerned primarily with how and why materially weak non-state actors sometimes defeat strong state actors (Mack 1975). The paradigm in conventional warfare is that the side with the better technology, material resources, superior population, territory, industrial resources, finances, and economic power is the stronger side and has the advantage (Record 2007). However, Record's research contrasts this paradigm to situations where states fight non-state actors, particularly states fighting internal and external insurgencies (Record 2007). Record distinguishes conventional warfare from counterinsurgency on the basis of the asymmetric nature of insurgency. He concludes that most states that lose to insurgencies suffer from some combination of inferior political will, inferior strategy, and an inability to isolate insurgent forces from external support (Record 2007).[2] Record's work is informative because he describes the

---

[2]Record acknowledges that small wars often evolve from asymmetric to symmetric, e.g., revolutions following a Maoist revolutionary war theory.

political aspects of asymmetrical conflict and takes asymmetry beyond the discussion of resources.

Similarly, Patricia Sullivan focuses on how the nature of a strong state's objectives affects the level of prewar uncertainty about the cost of attaining those objectives through the use of military force (2007, 497). She concludes that the primary determinant of success for strong states in armed conflict is the degree to which preconflict expectations about the cost of attaining objectives match the actual cost incurred during the conflict. Sullivan's work is informative because it shows that accurately assessing the probability of success is more difficult when a state's objective is to obtain political concessions or lack of resolve on the part of the enemy rather than the defeat of his armed forces.

Hence, the insurgency literature allows us to conclude that insurgency differs from conventional armed conflict in several significant ways. Namely, insurgency is political in its nature, in part, because of the means in which it is contested. Moreover, its nature is political because of the structure of the conflict (its asymmetry) and its purpose (controlling the population). As a result, scholars and practitioners have devised counterinsurgency theories that address these factors.

Counterinsurgency Theories

Scholars divide counterinsurgency theory into two primary perspectives: population-centric and enemy-centric.[3] However, a detailed review of the literature

---

[3]For a discussion on an alternative perspective, see Mark Moyar, *A Question of Command: Counterinsurgency from the Civil War to Iraq* (New Haven, CT: Yale University Press, 2009). Moyar defines counterinsurgency as a contest between elites in

reveals that the divisions are more complex and varied than a simple bifurcation.

Killcullen explains that the two approaches differ fundamentally because of their primary

tasks (2009). Enemy-centric approach assumes killing insurgents is the key task;

population-centric approach center focuses on protecting local people and gaining their

support (Killcullen 2009, 129-30).

Population-centric Counterinsurgency

Population-centric approach is less like conventional warfare and more like police

work: police patrolling to prevent violent crime (Killcullen 2009, 130). Of note,

population-centric theory assumes that insurgencies represent a contest for the loyalty of

the majority of uncommitted populace that could side with either the government or the

insurgents. Thus, success requires persuading this uncommitted populace to side with the

government or, at the very least, remain neutral.

Gompert and Gordon illustrate the population-centric theory itself is not unified,

and suggest three separate approaches: rational actor, hearts and minds, and

transformation (2008, 90). Similarly, Austin Long also distinguishes between the rational

actor and hearts and minds approach (2006). The rational actor approach seeks to shape

the incentives available to both the population and insurgents, i.e., the approach holds

that the government can effectively punish bad and reward good behavior. In this way,

populations are viewed as rational actors that will respond in more or less predictable

---

which the elite with superiority in certain leadership attributes usually wins. However,
Moyar's perspective is better understood as illustrating how effective leadership in a
population-centric counterinsurgency enhances the likelihood of success, rather than
leadership as a distinct counterinsurgency theory.

ways to incentives and sanctions from the competing insurgents and counterinsurgents (Long 2006, 24-25).

The hearts and minds approach sets out to win the population's allegiance by the government providing the population with the things they want so that a bond forms and the population will shun the insurgents. Long found that developed states had several years to adjust to the negative consequences of economic development; however, rapidly developing states lacked this adjustment period (2006, 25). Thus, government institutions in rapidly developing states could not keep pace with societal change, leading to disorder and instability. Insurgents could take advantage by promising alternative to the incumbent government. The hearts and mind approach provides an answer by offering to restore the hope of the people and gain their support for the government. In order to do this, it provides the people security from predation by insurgent forces. Moreover, it attempts to decrease the negative consequences of development and increasing positive aspects (Long 2006, 22-23).

Lastly, the transformation approach seeks to change the underlying structure of society and governance to make insurgency an irrelevant way of pursuing a grievance. This is accomplished by changing the societal institutions and structures, e.g., the justice system, so that grievances can be accommodated through nonviolent means (Gompert and Gordon 2008, 90-92).

The focus of each of the three aforementioned population-centric approaches remains the population; the difference lies with the way in which the counterinsurgent interprets the environment or conceptualizes the insurgency. Nevertheless, it is reasonable to assume that population-centric counterinsurgency operations would likely combine all three approaches to some degree. Moreover, killing and capturing insurgents is not relegated only to the enemy-centric theory (discussed below), but remains an important objective in all three population-centric approaches. However, population-centric theory rests upon the belief that long-term success comes from gaining and maintaining popular support.

Enemy-centric Counterinsurgency

In contrast to the population-centric theory of counterinsurgency, the enemy-centric theory focuses primarily on combating the insurgents and seeking to eliminate their organizations. The enemy-centric approach conceptualizes counterinsurgency as a contest with an organized enemy and focuses counterinsurgency operations on the insurgent organizations (Merom 2003). Focused on examining violent responses to insurgents, Merom describes three approaches of enemy-centric counterinsurgency theory: security forces can annihilate the popular base of insurgency, isolate the population from the insurgents, or selectively eradicate the insurgents and their leaders. Common to each variant is the readiness of the counterinsurgent to resort to violence against a civilian population. Merom further found that this violence indeed is both effective and efficient, because it reduces the amount of human and material resources invested and lost in conquest and pacification (Merom 2003, 46-47). I return the concept of effective and efficient violence in chapter 4 when discussing the factors that encourage security forces to use indiscriminate violence during counterinsurgency operations.

Understandably, the population- and enemy-centric approaches are often blurred when the operational environment is complex. This is especially true when counterinsurgency operations coincide with counter-terrorism operations. Thus, it is

15

worthwhile to distinguish counterinsurgency and counterterrorism. Specifically, exploring this dynamic complexity is helpful to understanding why counterinsurgent forces intermix what otherwise appear to be population- and enemy-centric approaches.

Counterterrorism

Killcullen uses the pre-surge Iraq War to illustrate the significance of distinguishing counterinsurgency and counterterrorism, explaining that Iraq consisted of four strategic problems (2009). First, there was an underlying capacity-building problem resulting from Iraq being a weak and fragile state. In addition, there were three overlapping security problems: terrorism and the presence of terrorists seeking to exploit instability; insurgency from a Sunni rebellion against the post-Saddam government and a Shi'a radical rebellion against authority; and a sectarian, ethnic conflict between Sunni and Shi'a and between Kurds, Arabs, Turkmen, and other ethnic groups (Killcullen 2009, 149-50). Thus, Killcullen found that Iraq was not a pure insurgency problem but a "hybrid war" requiring an approach that he labeled "counterinsurgency plus" (Killcullen 2009, 152). Killcullen believed that counterinsurgency theory alone did not provide a comprehensive answer. Rather, he advocated for operations that integrated counterinsurgency, counterterrorism, border security, nation-building, and peace enforcement operations, although he believed that effective counterinsurgency was the primary component for success (Killcullen 2009, 152).

David Ucko makes similar distinctions. Counterterrorism operations are different because they do not necessarily involve the creation of a new political order or the sustained presence of ground troops (Ucko 2009, 10). Ucko believes that the U.S. military interprets counterterrorism as enemy-centered and counterinsurgency as

16

population-centered. U.S. Army Field Manual 3-24 provides support for his conclusion in that it embraces the population-centric theory. Specifically, it lists several principles such as the need to foster legitimate governance, the centrality of politics, the importance of unity of effort, the need to operate according to the rule of law, and the need to separate insurgents from the populace, all of which follow the population-centric theory (FM 3-4 2006).

Therefore, Ucko finds that this distinction makes these two types of operations highly incongruent, though counterterrorism will often feature as one component of a wider counterinsurgency campaign (2009, 11). He further explains that even though past counterinsurgency experiences are varied with unique political setting and circumstances, we have derived common variables, such as the importance of achieving a nuanced political understanding of the campaign, operating under unified command, using intelligence to guide operations, isolating insurgents from the population, using the minimum amount of force necessary to achieve security, and assuring and maintaining the perceived legitimacy of the counterinsurgency effort in the eyes of the populace (Ucko 2009, 11). Ucko believes that while some of these experiences are "commonsensical," they provide insight into the "elusive logic of these operations and how significantly they differ from exclusively combat oriented campaigns" (Ucko 2009, 11).

Lastly, Gompert and Gordon posit an inclusive framework of categorizing insurgencies that explains that terrorist acts may often be part of a larger insurgent movement. Specifically, they categorize insurgencies into four categories: (1) local,

17

(2) local with international support, (3) global-local insurgency, and (4) global insurgency.

They define a local insurgency as an insurgency that is essentially self-contained in cause, conduct, scope, and effects. An example is the Philippines insurgency of 1899–1902 that the United States faced after the Spanish-American War. The goals of the insurgents were local and circumscribed, there were no outside forces or ideologies at play, and the stakes for international security were minimal (Gompert and Gordon 2008, 25). A local-international insurgency differs in that it finds external support in the form of money, arms, expertise, media attention, fighters, and propaganda both advantageous and indispensable. Nevertheless, the course and outcome of this type of insurgency will be decided by local factors, local insurgents, and the local population (Gompert and Gordon 2008, 26). A global-local insurgency also embraces external support; however, it transforms when the local insurgency becomes part of a wider regional or global struggle (Gompert and Gordon 2008, 27). Gompert and Gordon determined that this occurred in Iraq and Afghanistan, where jihadist motives and methods entered and altered local political (Sunni Baathist and Pashtun tribal, respectively) agendas. Thus, what may start as a localized power struggle can become much more difficult to quell when transnational networks and seemingly nonnegotiable causes, such as religion, affect local dynamics (Gompert and Gordon 2008, 27). Lastly, a global insurgency targets not only states but also systems of states. Some such movements preceded globalization, e.g., the anarchist movement and pre-Bolshevik international communist movement.

In sum, U.S. doctrine promotes population-centric counterinsurgency theory; however, the complex operational environment can cause U.S. forces to also conduct simultaneous counterterrorism operations in the same area of operations. Additionally, although different in purpose, enemy-centric counterinsurgency and counterterrorism are similar in practice. As a result, the U.S. can also blend population- and enemy-centric approaches.

Legitimacy and the Power to Coerce

As discussed above, the enemy-centric approach posits killing insurgents is the key counterinsurgency task; population-centric approach, the approach codified in U.S. Army doctrine, focuses on protecting local people and gaining their support. Thus, I now focus more precisely on the population-centric objective of protecting and gaining the support of the local populace.

Both insurgent and counterinsurgent have two tools in the struggle for control and support of the populace: a credible power to coerce and popular perceptions of legitimacy (Tovo 2006). The target of coercion, the populace, defines the threat's credibility, not the employer of the threat (Tovo 2006, 25). Consequently, conventional military power does not necessarily equate to credible coercive power. Recall that the asymmetric advantages of conventional forces, e.g., resources, technology, often results in overwhelming destructive power. Nevertheless, if the populace believes this conventional power will not, or cannot, be used for or against them, it has limited coercive value. This is particularly evident if the insurgent has demonstrated the ability to locate and punish noncompliant members of the populace and reward supporters (Tovo 2006, 25).

Of importance is the potential of force both to weaken and strengthen insurgency. Insurgents use force to weaken the state's ability to function and the population's confidence in the state's ability to provide security (Gompert and Gordon 2008, 32). As stated above, most people in an area threatened by an insurgency are probably not strongly motivated by either the insurgent cause or enthusiasm for the government. They want to be neither threatened by insurgents nor exposed to heavy-handed government security forces. But failure to protect the population can make it vulnerable to coercion by the insurgents and, therefore, less confident of and less inclined to cooperate with government authorities and security forces (Gompert and Gordon 2008, 32). It can also lead the population to conclude that the insurgents will eventually defeat and destroy the government, making that very outcome more likely (Gompert and Gordon 2008, 33).

At the same time, the use of force by the state has an inherent potential to strengthen or weaken legitimacy (Gompert and Gordon 2008, 33).[4] A legitimate government derives its power from the governed and competently manages collective security and political, economic, and social development (FM 3-24 2006; Cohen et al. 2006). Legitimate governments are inherently stable. They engender the popular support required to manage internal problems, change, and conflict, while illegitimate governments are inherently unstable (FM 3-24 2006; Cohen et al. 2006, 49). Misguided, corrupt, and incompetent governance inevitably fosters instability. An important contributing factor to the fostering of legitimate governance concerns the extent to which force should be used by security forces (Kitson 1991; Joes 2006). Thus, a critical measure of legitimacy, both theoretically and empirically, is the ability of a government to guarantee the security of its population (Galula 1964).

[4]Consider John A. Nevin's findings in the field of behavior science that retaliation by security forces to terrorist attacks does not result in a long term reduction in terrorist activity. Nevin posits that repeated retaliation might suppress terrorist attacks; however, severe or prolonged retaliation might also increase terrorist attacks (Nevin 2003).

For civilized states, the risk of strengthening insurgency by damaging legitimacy is especially high if (1) the insurgency is embedded in the population, (2) the insurgency already enjoys some popular sympathy, (3) force is not used with great care, or (4) foreign troops use force on the state's behalf (Gompert and Gordon 2008, 62). This risk is present, because of the risk that deadly force and intimidation will so alienate the population that its support for the insurgency rises and that recruiting outpaces losses. This will require the security forces to "maintain or establish good relations with the population to be mobilized into militia units, and above all, to employ only conservative military tactics in populated areas" (Joes 2006, 42). Support of the population is conditional (Galula 1964). Failing to use rectitude generates sympathy and recruits for the insurgency and erodes military discipline in foreign and host nation counterinsurgency forces (Joes 2006, 157-60).

This suggests that successful insurgency is unlikely when a state possesses security forces that are competent and loyal to the government (Joes 2006, 41). "Generally speaking, we may say that no revolution is even possible where the authority of the body politic is truly intact, and this means, under modern conditions, where the armed forces can be trusted to obey the civil authorities" (Arendt 1965, 40). This is especially the case in countries where state security forces have a history of brutalizing the people on behalf of the government (Gompert and Gordon 2008, 33). This is not to say that brutal force cannot be used effectively; it has been successful in defeating several insurgencies (e.g., Russia in Chechnya and Saddam Hussein in various Kurdish and Shi'a uprisings). But states that use such methods have little or no legitimacy to lose and thus no concern with its loss (Gompert and Gordon 2008, 34).

21

Rule of Law

Although rule of law theorists insist that the rule of law is essential to the success of any intervention in a failed or fragile state, there is a great divergence in scholarship regarding its meaning. The academic debate over the meaning ranges from desirable and measurable attributes (e.g. comprehensive laws, competent courts, etc.) to desirable policy end states (e.g. upholding law and order, making predictable judgments regarding conduct, etc.).

Accordingly, some theorists advocate an approach to the rule of law that focuses on the structural aspects rather than the substantive content of laws. In other words, these minimalist theorists hold that the rule of law is "the law of rules" (Scalia 1989), i.e., rule of law involves rules and practices that are routinely followed. Others advocate for the importance of law being universal in form, consistently applied, and sufficiently well known that citizens can plan their lives around them (Waldron 2002). Still others emphasize the importance of "*process* to the rule of law, insisting that the rule of law involves and requires accessible, transparent mechanisms for legal and political change" (Stromseth et al. 2006, 70, emphasis in original; Posner 2003).

In contrast, substantive rule of law theorists acknowledge the importance of the laws structure and components, but insist that the true rule of law also requires particular substantive commitments, e.g., the protection of human rights, minority rights, justice, equality, and freedom (Summers 1993).

Others advocate for a synergistic approach that emphasizes means and ends (Stromseth et al. 2006, 80). This approach explicitly recognizes the need for multiple, mutually reinforcing reforms that are carefully attuned to strengthening cultural and political as well as institutional foundations for the rule of law (Stromseth et al. 2006). Thus, reformers must be clear in the rule of law goals they seek to achieve and not attempt to simply build institutions. There is merit in each approach, but that debate is outside the scope of this thesis.

Notwithstanding the variance in rule of law theory, there is popular agreement regarding several basic tenets that together describe the rule of law for our purpose. The seminal work is offered by Richard Fallon, who describes these views. First, the rule of law must incorporate rules, standards, and principles to assist people in conducting their lives. Second, the rule of law should have efficacy, i.e., it should actually guide an individual's actions. Third, the rule of law must provide stability in order to facilitate planning and coordination over time. Fourth, the rule of law requires that legal authority is supreme over the whims of those in power. Lastly, the rule of law provides impartiality, so that enforcement of the law and fair and unbiased (Fallon 1997). Under these precepts, the rule of law refers to a principle of governance in which all actors are accountable and acquiescent to laws that are neither arbitrary nor capricious.

However, this representation fails to address various substantive elements that U.S. Army doctrine incorporates. The U.S. Army doctrine defines the rule of law as the following: "rule of law is a principle of governance in which all persons, institutions and entities, public and private, including the state itself, are accountable to laws that are publically promulgated, equally enforced, and independently adjudicated, and which are consistent with international human rights principles" (FM 3-07 2008; CLAMO 2011).

In addition to this doctrinal definition, FM 3-07 and the *Rule of Law Handbook* also incorporate several other concepts into a working rule of law concept for use in stability operations. First, U.S. Army doctrine includes the concept that only the state monopolizes the use of force in the resolution of disputes (FM 3-07 2008; CLAMO 2011). This is not to say that non-state entities are excluded from using force; however, the state must be able to retain ultimate control by effectively regulating other entities. Additionally, U.S. Army doctrine incorporates the concepts that individuals are secure in their person and property (FM 3-07 2008; CLAMO 2011). The addition of these elements is in accordance with the previously discussed literature regarding power and legitimacy.

Importantly, the U.S. doctrine also requires that the state protect basic human rights (FM 3-07 2008; CLAMO 2011). This substantive addition is problematic, because it places at issue exactly what rights the law must protect for a society to be considered governed by the rule of law. Some scholars define this obligation as those relating to equal treatment as espoused in international treaty (CLAMO 2011).[5] Nevertheless, it would be equally problematic to ignore a state's obligation to protect human rights. For example, consider a state that adheres to other rule of law principles, but considers a segment of its population to be personal property. Intuitively, it would be difficult to conclude that such a state was adhering to the rule of law. Therefore, this implies that human rights must be considered. It also implies that these rights may be those not already observed or accepted by the society in question.[6] Consequently, I find that the

---

[5]For examples, see the Universal Declaration of Human Rights of 1948 and the International Covenant on Civil and Political Rights of 1966.

[6]Support for this perspective is found in the post-conflict reconstruction literature. Particularly, post-conflict reconstruction requires a state to be minimally capable in four areas: security, governance and participation, social and economic well-being, and justice and reconciliation (Orr 2004, 11). Relevant to the rule of law, a state with a capable justice and reconciliation system includes impartiality and accountability, transparency,

protection of human rights for the purposes of this thesis; however, I acknowledge that this is contestable.

Thus, U.S. Army doctrine, expressed in FM 3-07 and the *Rule of Law Handbook*, incorporates the views of minimalist, substantive, and synergistic rule of law theorists and concludes that the rule of law exists in a society when seven factors are met:

1. The state monopolizes the use of force in the resolution of disputes.

2. Individuals are secure in their persons and property.

3. The state is bound by law and does not act arbitrarily.

4. The law can be readily determined and is stable enough to allow individuals to plan their affairs.

5. Individuals have meaningful access to an effective and impartial justice system.

6. The state protects basic human rights and fundamental freedoms.

7. Individuals rely on the existence of justice institutions and the content of law in the conduct of their daily lives. (FM 3-07 2008; CLAMO 2011)[7]

Nevertheless, these principles are not contained in the U.S. Army's seminal doctrine regarding counterinsurgency, FM. 3-24. U.S. Army counterinsurgency doctrine

---

fairness, humane treatment, and formal and informal grievance procedures (Orr 2004, 11).

[7]These effects are largely derived from Jane Stromseth, David Wippman, and Rosa Brooks, *Can Might Make Rights?: Building the Rule of Law After Military Interventions* (Stromseth et al. 2006, 78). Of note, the *Rule of Law Handbook* substitutes the work "legal" for "justice" in the fifth principle. Notwithstanding the change terminology, the explanatory text indicates that this principle refers to both formal institutions for enforcing civil and criminal laws, including courts, corrections, and police, and informal grievance mechanisms that operate in accordance with cultural norms.

describes "key aspects of the rule of law" without reconciling them with the foregoing list. Specifically, FM 3-24, states that the rule of law includes the following:

1. A government that derives its powers from the governed and competently manages, coordinates, and sustains collective security, as well as political, social, and economic development. This includes local, regional, and national government.

2. Sustainable security institutions. These include a civilian-controlled military as well as police, court, and penal institutions. The latter should be perceived by the local populace as fair, just, and transparent.

3. Fundamental human rights. (FM 3-24 2006)

Importantly, FM 3-24 is internally inconsistent regarding these "key aspects" of the rule of law. Specifically, the manual makes myriad references within the text in general that support and compliment the rule of law framework described in FM 3-07 and the *Rule of Law Handbook*, e.g., requiring the state retain the monopoly on the use of force, requiring security forces to use force only discriminately, and promoting rule of law institution. I will address the incongruity present in U.S. Army doctrine in chapter 4.

Causal Framework

Craig Parsons proposes a typology to describe the relationship between four types of explanatory factors in political analysis: structural, institutional, ideational and psychological (Parsons 2007). Specifically, structural and institutional explanations feature a logic-of-position that "explains by detailing the landscape around someone to show how an obstacle course of material or manmade constraints and incentives channels her to certain actions" (Parsons 2007, 13). The term "material" refers to structural causal factors like a distribution of wealth, or a distribution of physical power, while the term "institutional" refers to human-made factors and within path-dependent processes

(Parsons 2007, 12-13). Conversely, ideational and psychological explanations are characterized by a logic-of-interpretation, which "explains by showing that someone arrives at an action only through one interpretation of what is possible and/or desirable" (Parsons 2007, 13). The key difference between ideational and psychological forces is that the former are historical and social constructions while the later are embedded in hard-wired mental processes.

The four factors are helpful to the analysis of security forces' adherence to the rule of law. Intuitively, security forces should conduct operations in accordance with the rule of law if doing so enhances likelihood of success. Yet, we know empirically that security forces do not always adhere to these principles. Thus, it is informative to explore whether or not there are hidden or counterintuitive causal factors that obstruct security forces from conducting operations in this matter. Understanding these factors in the context provided by Parsons allows for a richer understanding of the dynamics that reduce government legitimacy and hinder counterinsurgency efforts.

Conclusion

I reviewed in this chapter several areas of counterinsurgency literature to allow for a focused examination of the conduct of security forces in relation to the rule of law. Specifically, scholars have concluded that the nature of insurgency is political. Consequently, there are two viable theories in which to respond. The population-centric approach makes competition for the allegiance of the population the foremost objective. In contrast, the enemy-centric approach makes annihilating the insurgents or their support through violence the foremost objective. Concentrating on population-centric counterinsurgency, the approach favored by U.S. doctrine and practice, I identified two mechanisms that scholars believe insurgents and counterinsurgents use to persuade the population–credible coercive power and popular perceptions of legitimacy. Lastly, I reviewed the various rule of law theories as they apply to counterinsurgency.

Using this review of counterinsurgency and rule of law literature, I advocate in chapter 4 for rule of law framework for that appropriate for security forces conducting counterinsurgency operations. I then apply this framework to the counterinsurgency literature and conclude that both foreign and host nation security forces are more successful at counterinsurgency if they conduct operations in accordance with the rule of law. Lastly, I identify several hidden causal factors that influence security forces to conduct operations that that both support and conflict with rule of law principles and describe them by causal logic, e.g., institutional, structural, ideational, and psychological.

CHAPTER 3

RESEARCH METHODOLOGY

I explain in this chapter the methodology used to address the primary research question and I explain the conceptual design of the methodology. This is a descriptive study on counterinsurgency and rule of law theory. The research I describe in this study is based solely on qualitative research methods.

First, I focus on the political nature of insurgency in order to later explain the relevance of the rule of law to counterinsurgency operations. Additionally, I incorporate works regarding asymmetry, which is concerned with how and why materially weak non-state actors are able to defeat materially strong state actors.

Second, I conduct a comprehensive review of counterinsurgency theory and determine that there are only two widely accepted theories: population-centric and enemy-centric. I compare and contrast these theories and to explore the related concept of counterterrorism. As a result, I illustrate that current U.S. doctrine favors population-centric counterinsurgency, but that all three theories are blended in practice.

Third, I survey the population-centric counterinsurgency literature that security force use two instruments to achieve this objective: the use of credible power to coerce and the ability to foster perceptions of legitimate governance. Further, examine how these two instruments were incorporated into U.S. Army counterinsurgency doctrine.

Fourth, I identify and describe the pertinent aspects of the competing rule of law theories by surveying and summarizing the three principal rule of law theoretical schools–minimalist, substantivist, and synergist. This provides the theoretical basis to compare U.S. Army rule of law and counterinsurgency doctrine.

Lastly, I introduce a typology constructed by political theorist Craig Parsons, which describes the use of four causal logics–structural, institutions, ideational, and psychological. My recitation of Parsons' typology allows for the causal factors that emerged from the review of the counterinsurgency and rule of law literature to be categorized and described in an approach not attempted elsewhere in military scholarship.

CHAPTER 4

ANALYSIS

This chapter consists of three sections. First, I utilize the counterinsurgency and rule of law literature described in chapter 2 to explain why U.S. Army rule of law doctrine contained in FM 3-07 and the *Rule of Law Handbook* is more suitable for counterinsurgency than the current rule of law doctrine contained in FM 3-24. Second, I describe why security forces that follow the rule of law are more likely to defeat an armed insurgency. Lastly, I identify and describe several hidden or counterintuitive factors that influence counterinsurgency forces from following the rule of law.

A Rule of Law Framework for Counterinsurgency

The literature discussed in chapter 2 illustrates that there is much debate between theorists regarding the definition of the rule of law. Nevertheless, there are several aspects of the rule of law that are widely accepted. As described in chapter 2, these concepts are captured thoroughly by U.S. Army doctrine contained in FM 3-07 and the *Rule of Law Handbook* (CLAMO 2011). Unfortunately, the U.S. Army's seminal doctrine regarding counterinsurgency, FM. 3-24, adopts a rule of law position that in internally inconsistent and in conflict with FM 3-07 and the *Rule of Law Handbook*. In this section I will describe in more detail why FM 3-24's rule of law position is inconsistent and inappropriate for counterinsurgency.

Recall that the counterinsurgency literature illustrates that the nature of insurgency is political. Under the population-centric theory of counterinsurgency, obtaining the support or neutrality of the population is the key objective. Security forces attain this objective through the use of two instruments: the credible power to coerce and the popular perceptions of legitimacy. As described in chapter 2, U.S. Army doctrine embraces population-centric counterinsurgency and incorporates the tenets of this theory within FM 3-24.

Nonetheless, FM 3-24 posits three "key aspects" of the rule of law, two of which are unsuitable for security forces conducting counterinsurgency operations. Specifically, FM 3-24 states that the rule of law should include the following:

1. A government that derives its powers from the governed and competently manages, coordinates, and sustains collective security, as well as political, social, and economic development. This includes local, regional, and national government.

2. Sustainable security institutions. These include a civilian-controlled military as well as police, court, and penal institutions. The latter should be perceived by the local populace as fair, just, and transparent.

3. Fundamental human rights. (FM 3-24 2006)

The first two aspects are problematic in that they unnecessarily incorporate a substantive rule of law view that is exceptionally expansive. I described in chapter 2 that substantive rule of law theorists advocate that the rule of law should incorporate substantive aspirations. However, the inclusion of substantive principles creates two difficulties.

First, it places at issue exactly what rights the law must protect. Thus, counterinsurgency forces (or their sponsoring state) must determine the relative value of these competing rights, select which are applicable to the given context, and then incorporate those rights into its military operations. Second, substantive theory implies that these rights may be those not already observed or accepted in a given society. Thus, counterinsurgency forces may find themselves promoting rights and values inapposite to the indigenous society.

This is less problematic when security forces seek to promote substantive rights or principles that are generally accepted. For example, the desire to incorporate the protection of basic human rights and freedoms is generally acceptable. It is also arguable that the need to protect basic human rights and freedoms is necessary for any state to exist under the rule of law. Consider the example described in chapter 2, in which a state that adheres to other rule of law principles, but considers a segment of its population to be personal property. Intuitively, it would be difficult to conclude that such a state was adhering to the rule of law.

Yet, FM 3-24 seeks to incorporate a much too expansive view of substantive rule of law principles, e.g., positing the necessity for a republican form of government and an American civil-military tradition. Substantive rule of law theorists would approve of this approach, as they believe the rule of law must include protections such as "rules securing minimum welfare . . . , rules securing some variety of the market economy, rules protecting at least some basic human rights, and rules institutionalizing democratic governance" (Summers 1993). However, it is indisputable that the foregoing principles espouse a bold substantive view of the rule of law, which, as described in chapter 2, is not the position of the majority of rule of law scholars.

Promoting these substantive principles as state policy may have merit, but that debate immaterial to this discussion. Significantly, incorporating them into a rule of law framework is problematic. This nuance is recognized in several passages throughout FM

3-24, which taken in its entirety supports the conclusion that legitimate governance is possible in states without a non-Western tradition.

Alternatively, U.S. Army doctrine, expressed in FM 3-07 and the *Rule of Law Handbook*, incorporates a more universal concept of the rule of law and avoids mandating controversial substantive rule of law principles. Under this framework, the rule of law exists in a society when seven factors are met:

1. The state monopolizes the use of force in the resolution of disputes.

2. Individuals are secure in their persons and property.

3. The state is bound by law and does not act arbitrarily.

4. The law can be readily determined and is stable enough to allow individuals to plan their affairs.

5. Individuals have meaningful access to an effective and impartial justice system.

6. The state protects basic human rights and fundamental freedoms.

7. Individuals rely on the existence of justice institutions and the content of law in the conduct of their daily lives. (FM 3-07 2008; CLAMO 2011)

As explained in chapter 2, this framework is suitable for use for security forces conducting counterinsurgency operations because if comprehensively incorporates the concepts of population-centric counterinsurgency. For example, consider the concept of individuals being secure in their persons and property. A critical objective of population-centric counterinsurgency theory is the ability of a government to guarantee the security of its population. As the counterinsurgency literature instructs, the support or neutrality of the population toward the incumbent regime is conditional and the failure to protect the population can make the state vulnerable to coercion by insurgents.

As such, population-centric counterinsurgency theory requires that the rule of law restrict the extent and manner in which force in used. In order to adhere to this principle security forces must refrain from using coercive power unless properly sanctioned by the state, e.g., for the purpose of securing the population. Additionally, security forces must refrain from misusing the power to coerce by constraining the means in which they employ force.

Similarly, this approach also includes the concept that only the state monopolizes the use of force in the resolution of disputes. This is squarely in accordance with the rule of law, as "[i]t is impossible to say that a society is governed by the [rule of law] if compulsion is not the sole province of the state" (CLAMO 2011).

To summarize, the U.S. Army doctrinal "key aspects" of establishing the rule of law expressed in FM 3-24 are unsuitable and contrary to counterinsurgency and rule of law theory. Moreover, these "key aspects" are internally inconsistent with the text of FM 3-24. Alternatively, the framework expressed in FM 3-07 and the *Rule of Law Handbook* provides an appropriate and useful tool to further evaluate whether following the rule of law assists security forces to defeat an armed insurgency.

In this section I examine the existing U.S. Army doctrinal framework for the rule of law and conclude that the rule of law framework contained in FM 3-07 and the *Rule of Law Handbook* is more useful in the counterinsurgency context. In the next section I describe how following rule of law principles influence security forces' operations and conclude that following the rule of law assists security forces to defeat armed insurgency.

Following the Rule of Law Assists Security
Forces Defeat Armed Insurgency

We know from the insurgency literature discussed in chapter 2 that the very nature of insurgency is political. Insurgents seek to replace an existing order with one that conforms to their political, economic, ideological, or religious vision by using political resources and instruments of violence against the incumbent government. Population-centric counterinsurgency theory responds to these dynamics by making the indigenous population the object of the conflict. Thus, success in population-centric counterinsurgency requires security forces to persuade this uncommitted populace to side with the indigenous government or, at the very least, remain neutral. Security forces accomplish this objective by employing two instruments of counterinsurgency warfare: the credible power to coerce and popular perception of legitimacy (Tovo 2006). Therefore, security forces should be more successful at conducting counterinsurgency operations if conducting those operations in accordance with the rule of law furthers their ability to use credible coercive power or foster popular perceptions of legitimacy. In the following two sections, I analyze the relationship between the rule of law and both instruments.

Rule of Law and Coercive Power

The literature regarding asymmetric warfare informs us that conventional military power does not equate to credible coercive power. While resource and technological superiority may provide definitive destructive advantages that equate to defeating an armed force, they do not equate to definitive advantages when the objective is to obtain political concessions or defeat an enemy's resolve. The counterinsurgent's ability to wield coercive power becomes credible only when and if the population perceives it to be so, i.e., when the population perceives that the power can be used for or against them. In relation to counterinsurgency security forces, this relates to the exercise of power through constructive or destructive force.

However, the use of force carries with it the potential to both weaken and strengthen the insurgency. Population-centric counterinsurgency theory posits that the majority of the populace in a contested area threatened by an insurgency is not strongly motivated by either the insurgent cause or enthusiasm for the incumbent regime. This contested majority desires to be neither threatened by insurgents nor exposed to oppressive government security forces. Therefore, the critical contributing factor to the efficacy of security forces' use of coercive power is the extent and means to which force is used or abused. In other words, security forces use coercive power more effectively when they avoid using the power abusively. They do this by practicing rectitude and avoiding the indiscriminate use of force – concepts manifested within the aforementioned rule of law framework.

Specifically, one tenet of the rule of law framework is that individuals are secure in their person and property. Security forces that practice rectitude and avoid the indiscriminate use of force squarely adhere to this principle. This is particularly evident in societies with a low or nonexistent rule of law tradition in which the primary protection to be offered by the rule of may be protection from the state itself (CLAMO 2011, 5).

Second, another tenet of the rule of law is that the state is itself bound by law and does not act arbitrarily. Security forces that practice rectitude and avoid the

37

indiscriminate use of force demonstrate to the populace that the state itself in constrained in the manner and extent in which it uses its monopoly of force. "In enforcing the law, the [state] must be prevented from acting with complete autonomy to achieve its chosen end lest order be obtained through terror or intimidation, which would not be an exercise of the rule of law" (CLAMO 2011, 5).

Lastly, a third relevant tenet of the rule of law is that states respect basic human rights and freedoms. As an extension of the state, security forces respect basic human rights when they practice rectitude and avoid the indiscriminate use of force. Though different societies to define rights in different ways, even a minimalist rule of law approach to including substantive rights requires that states respect core principles such as prohibitions against racial, ethnic, religious and gender discrimination, torture, slavery, prolonged arbitrary detentions, and extrajudicial killings (Stromseth 2008, 79).

Counterinsurgency scholars have yet to expressly acknowledge the causal link between coercive power and the rule of law. Nevertheless, they universally conclude that security forces are more successful if they practice rectitude and avoid the use of indiscriminate force[8] (Joes 2006; Record 2007; O'Neill 2005; Galula 1964; Kitson 1991; Thompson 1966). Based on the foregoing analysis, it is also reasonable to conclude that security forces are more successful if they follow the rule of law.

The literature provides empirical examples of how the failure to use rectitude and discriminate power hinders counterinsurgency. For example, a U.S. Military Red Team

---

[8]This theoretical conclusion rests upon the assumption that the security forces are conducting operations in accordance with population-centric counterinsurgency theory. As explained in chapter 2, the indiscriminate use of force can be effective if security forces are conducting operations under enemy-centric theory.

study of Afghanistan National Security Forces (ANSF) in 2007, examined the perceptions of those forces towards U.S. operations. Of note, the study determined the following:

> The factors that fueled the most animosity included U.S. convoys not allowing traffic to pass, reportedly indiscriminant return [of] U.S. fire that caused civilian casualties, naively using flawed intelligence sources, U.S. Forces conducting night raids/home searches, violating female privacy during searches, and U.S. road massacres of civilians. (ANSF Study 2007)

In sum, security forces are more successful at conducting population-centric counterinsurgency when they conduct operations in accordance with the rule of law, because their coercive power is more credible when used with rectitude and used discriminately. As described below, the rule of law has the same positive effect upon security forces second instrument of warfare–legitimacy.

Rule of Law and Legitimacy

In the previous section, I described the interplay between the rule of law and the use of coercive power by counterinsurgency forces. Of note, I addressed population-centric counterinsurgency without distinguishing between the three approaches (hearts and minds, rational actor, transformation) delineated in the literature. I find this appropriate in that context, because the use of coercive power does not change under any of the three population-centric approaches. However, considering each population-centric approach is helpful to addressing the relationship between the rule of law and legitimacy, because concepts of legitimacy are nuanced under each approach.

Hearts and Minds

First, recall that the crux of the hearts and minds approach is the ability of the counterinsurgent forces, as an extension of the government, to fulfill the promises made to the indigenous population so that hope is restored in the incumbent regime. Since the insurgents are also competing for the population by providing alternatives, counterinsurgency forces must simultaneously secure the population from insurgent predation while persuading it. As a result, successful hearts and mind counterinsurgency rests upon the ability of the counterinsurgent security forces to protect the population while simultaneously providing economic, political, and societal development and opportunity. As described above, one tenet of the rule of law framework is that individuals are secure in their person and property and it is easy to conclude that security forces that provide for the physical protection of the populace support the rule of law.

It is intuitive to consider the provision of security only in terms of its physical manifestation. In other words, protecting the population is commonly considered a matter of physically separating the population from the insurgents, protecting them from immediate and large-scale violence, and restoring the state's ability to maintain territorial integrity (Orr 2004). Yet, the political nature of insurgency implies that security forces must do more. The goal of security is also to protect the population from coercion by the insurgents and increase the likelihood that the population will cooperate with the government by fostering confidence in the incumbent regime (Gompert and Gordon 2008). This concept of security implies

> a condition of acceptable public safety, particularly the establishment of an
> environment where in citizens can conduct daily business relatively free from
> violence or coercion directed at them by the government, organized crime,
> political organizations, and ethnic groups . . . markets provide goods and services

40

without evading laws and regulations, an those laws and regulations are enforced objectively, with avenues of citizen recourse. (Orr 2004, 40-41)

It naturally follows that security forces that provide security under this expansive notion are adhering to the rule of law. This is not to say the physical security is not necessary; but, it is only one aspect of security. Security forces must also foster legitimacy through their support for the rule of law.

<u>Rational Actor</u>

Alternatively, security forces conducting operations under the rational actor approach seek to shape the incentives available to both the population and the insurgents. In other words, this approach requires that the government effectively punish bad and reward good behavior. In this way, populations react as rational actors by responding in fairly predictable ways to incentives and sanctions from the competing insurgents and counterinsurgents. Thus, successful rational actor counterinsurgency rests not with what incentives and sanctions security forces employ; rather, success is determined by how best to employ incentives and sanctions to influence the population's behavior.

With this in mind, consider the tensions that arose over the U.S. security forces' detention practices in Iraq, where Iraqi judges frequently complained that security forces detained Iraqi suspects that the judges had ordered released and released suspects that the judges had ordered detained (Stromseth et al. 2006, 323). Iraqi judges also complained that the security forces frequently failed to produce detainees for court proceedings as the judges requested.

Security forces defended their actions based on security concerns (convoys transporting detainees were frequently targeted by insurgents) or corruption (replacing their judgment for that of the Iraqi judges when they believed corruptive practices such as bribery or nepotism were behind the judges' rulings). In this manner, security forces were practicing rational actor counterinsurgency by seeking to influence the populations' practical choices, e.g., to reward good behavior (convoy protection, just judicial decisions) and punish bad behavior (lack of security, corruption). Yet, this fostered a perception in the indigenous population that security forces were unable or unwilling to cooperate with properly issued court orders (Stromseth et al. 2006, 323). This example illustrates that the manner in which incentives and sanctions are determined and employed affect legitimacy.

As a result, government legitimacy was undermined. Conversely, security forces foster legitimacy by employing incentives and sanctions that support the rule of law. The rule of law requires that the law be readily determined and is stable enough to allow individuals to plan their affairs. Societies provide stability not simply through the promulgation of laws and the maintenance of institutions. Instruments of society must genuinely and openly commit to adhering to the rule of law. "[The] rule of law involves not merely the existence of formal rules and rights but also the existence of people who voluntarily choose to respect those rules and rights, this definition emphasizes that the rule of law is a matter of cultural commitments as well as institutions and legal codes" (Stromseth et al. 2006, 78).

This is no different for a state's security forces, who must abide by the rule of law even when may be contrary to its own perceived, short-term self-interest.

<u>Transformational</u>

Lastly, security forces utilizing the transformational approach are likewise more successful when conforming to the rule of law. The transformation approach seeks to change the underlying structure of society and governance to make insurgency an irrelevant way of pursuing a grievance. This is accomplished by changing the societal institutions and structures–these are precisely the types of institutions involved in the rule of law. Improved law enforcement, judicial processes, and correctional systems provide mechanisms so that grievances can be accommodated through nonviolent means. For example, a well-functioning justice system enables persons to address grievances through criminal and civil courts (Gompert and Gordon 2008, 93).

In sum, security forces are more successful at conducting population-centric counterinsurgency when they conduct operations in accordance with the rule of law, because doing so fosters perceptions of legitimacy. This is accomplished under the hearts and mind approach through our expanded notion of security, under the rational actor approach through the employment of the proper incentives and sanctions, and under the transformational approach through the creation of alternative grievance mechanisms.

Having established that the rule of law positively affects counterinsurgency success, I now identify and describe why security forces might be hindered from adhering to the rule of law when conducting counterinsurgency.

Factors Influencing Whether Security Forces Follow the Rule of Law

In the first section of this chapter, I propose the adoption of a rule of law framework suitable for analyzing the conduct of security forces operating under population-centric counterinsurgency theory. In the second section of this chapter, I describe how the rule of law advantages security forces to conduct counterinsurgency operations given this rule of law framework and the counterinsurgency literature reviewed in chapter 2. Specifically, I focus on the two instruments of population-centric counterinsurgency warfare–the credible power to coerce and popular perceptions of legitimacy–and conclude that security forces utilize both instruments more effectively when conducting operations in accordance with the rule of law.

Assuming, *arguendo*, that this conclusion has merit, we would intuitively expect the security forces conducting counterinsurgency operations under the population-centric theory to adhere to the rule of law. Similarly, foreign security forces conducting security force assistance operations should also seek to influence host nation security forces to do the same.

Yet, we know empirically that security forces do not always adhere to these principles. For example, in Afghanistan, special operations units conducted direct action missions since 2002, with little effect upon the Taliban insurgency. These raids were conducted without consideration for their place within the larger counter insurgency and rule of law context. A senior U.S. military officer in Afghanistan reported in March 2009:

> I thought we could decapitate the insurgency. I was wrong. We've gone through twenty-two [high value targets] in the province, but [the insurgents] nominate someone new to take over the leadership very fast. The duration of our success is not more than three to four weeks before the insurgents have a new leader, and often that person is younger and more brutal. Even if someone killed [the head of the Pakistani Taliban], someone else will simply take over. (Rid et al. 2010, 132)

Similarly, security forces in Argentina conducted an indiscriminate campaign against the Montenegro and other insurgents, which created pressures on later governments to bring those responsible to trial (O'Neil 2005, 175). Consider also the Israeli operations against

44

Fedayeen during 1968-69. Reprisals began with Israeli civilians attacking Arab civilians after Palestinian terrorist attacks and spread to the Israeli security forces (O'Neil 2005, 176).[9]

Thus, in the remainder of this chapter I identify and describe how several hidden causal factors prevent security forces from conducting operations in accordance with the rule of law. I do not suggest that this list is exhaustive. I also recognize that other factors that may also influence security forces may be more apparent an easier to describe, e.g., insufficient training, lack of resources, etc. Rather, I intend to draw our attention on the causal factors that may otherwise go unnoticed. Attempting to understand these factors within the typology introduced in chapter 2 allows for a richer appreciation of the dynamics that influence counterinsurgency efforts.

Structural Logic

Structure is the first of Parsons' causal logics. At its core, structural logic is a logic-of-position. Individuals react regularly and reasonable to externally imposed factors. Structural claims explain these reactions as a direct function of a person's position in a material landscape that surrounds him. Parsons provides the metaphor of person maneuvering through an exogenous obstacle course of physical constraints and resources (Parsons 2007, 64). Geography, a distribution of wealth, and a distribution of physical power are examples of these material constraints and resources.

---

[9]Ultimately, the Israeli government took efforts to educate and such violence could lead victims to support the insurgents. Moreover, the Israeli government took active measures supporting the rule of law when several security forces were brought to trial and convicted for indiscriminately killings of Arabs (O'Neil 2005, 176).

Likewise, we can explain how security forces act towards the rule of law as a function of their position in the constraints and resources relevant to counterinsurgency. I describe below two structures affecting security forces ability to follow the rule of law: (1) a security forces' position relative to the indigenous population; and (2) organizational corruption within the security force.

Position Relative to the Indigenous Population

The requirement that security forces establish and maintain geographic proximity with the population is thoroughly addressed in the counterinsurgency literature and doctrine. However, this is not the only relevant concept of proximity. The counterinsurgency literature demonstrates that it is critical that military operations support and supplement clear political objectives. In the context of population-centric counterinsurgency, this requires security forces to maintain and establish good relations with the population. Therefore, it follows logically that the more security forces are able to empathize with the indigenous population the more likely they are to establish and maintain these relations and foster perceptions of legitimacy.

For this reason, we can explain why security forces act in accordance or discordance with the rule of law, in part, as a function of their position in relation to the indigenous population. I suggest that there are at least four such relationships: (1) national/local, (2) foreign/indigenous, (3) military/police, and (4) regular/irregular forces.

National or Local Forces

Local forces are inherently more closely connected to the population than national forces. This connection is a result of several factors, such as their intimate familiarity with the local inhabitants, terrain, tribal loyalties, and family relationships (Nagl 2005; Joes 2006). In this way, the relative position of local forces to the indigenous population provides them with several unique advantages in operating in accordance with the rule of law.

First, local forces can more effectively separate insurgents from the indigenous population, because of their increased familiarly with the local inhabitants and terrain. Second, local civilians that participate in their own self-defense become more attached to the official regime and, by implication, less sympathetic to the insurgent cause. Lastly, local forces can obtain intelligence through the public support that naturally adheres to them. Importantly, these factors increase the likelihood that local forces practice rectitude and constrain their use of force. This has been shown empirically, as local forces have historically been more conservative in the use of firepower (Joes 2006, 113).

Conversely, national forces are less likely to adhere to the rule of law because of their relative position to the indigenous population. In particular, national forces are less likely to have the depth of understanding of local patterns of behavior that is achievable by local forces. This exogenous constraint disadvantages national forces and results in an increased likelihood to use force indiscriminately.

Foreign or Indigenous Forces

The same structural advantages and constraints occur when foreign and indigenous forces are compared. The forces most connected to the population, generally

47

speaking, are those of the indigenous state who share values, beliefs, customs, and a societal or cultural narrative. The relative position of foreign forces to the indigenous population hinders them from operating in accordance with the rule of law, because they must maneuver through an obstacle course that they perceive as more complex and difficult. Namely, they interact with a population in which they do not share common values, beliefs, customs, and a societal or cultural narrative. This highlight the importance of building effective indigenous security forces through the conduct of security force assistance.

Nevertheless, indigenous forces are more likely than foreign forces to enjoy legitimacy only if (1) the government to which these services answer is seen as legitimate, effective, and independent (i.e., not a U.S. puppet); and (2) the services are trustworthy and competent (Gompert and Gordon 2008,81).

Military or Police

For various reasons, states may rely on military rather than police forces to conduct counterinsurgency. Yet, of the range of security forces, none is more critical than police to enforcing the rule of law. Although security is dependent on both military and policing forces, the imposition of order is not the provision of security (Orr 2004). Orr explains that the interplay between these two forces is important in any counterinsurgency operation, with the military focusing on the extraordinary event or threat and the police focusing on the internal, recurring, provision of public safety (Orr 2004, 43).

Police forces are inherently better for these operations, because they tend to minimize the use of force during operations (Gompert and Gordon 2008, 82). Police can be both more effective and more legitimate than military forces, especially if combined with fair, efficient, and transparent justice and penal systems. In comparison, military force, being inherently clumsier and more lethal, may intimidate more than reassure the population, especially when insurgents are hidden in urban areas.

The benefit provided to police by their relative position to the indigenous population is particularly evident when cultural barriers exist. Wrongful arrests and civilian casualties are inevitable when insurgents look like other military-age males (Gompert and Gordon 2008). Such mistakes further the separation between the indigenous government and the population and aid insurgent recruiting. Military forces are more likely to make deadly mistakes than police, who abide by rules of engagement designed to minimize violence.

This situation is further worsened when security has deteriorated to the point that ordinary police are inadequate. In these situations, experience indicates that it is better to use high-performance, quick-response forces skilled in both policing and light combat than to rely upon regular military security forces (Gompert and Gordon 2008, 82). These specialized, constabulary forces capable of both law enforcement and low-intensity operations, are more legitimate in the view of the population and more proficient than regular military security forces, at least against small insurgent concentrations. Regular military forces are inculcated with doctrine, training, and rules of engagement that are often unproductive and sometimes counterproductive in a struggle with insurgents in the midst of a contested population (Gompert and Gordon 2008).

Nevertheless, the use of police or constabulary forces is not of itself a guarantee that such forces will adhere to the rule of law. In many post-conflict states, police institutions that are closely associated with, or an outgrowth of, military security institutions are not integrated into a system of civil restarts and oversight (Orr 2004, 43). The development of the rule of law in these states is often hindered because law enforcement is handled by military forces instead of police, where the reconstruction of the judiciary, legal profession, humane correctional institutions, regulatory and oversight framework, and civil and property codes often languishes while the police operate as an extension of a military security force (Orr 2004).

Regular or Irregular

Insurgency theorists commonly discuss the requirement on the part of the insurgent to leverage time, space, and political will against the competing actions of the indigenous government (Galula 1962). For example, insurgents draw strength from having bases and safe areas to instigate attacks, development insurgent forces, coordinate political processes to put forward alternative governance, and hide from security forces to protract the conflict. Accordingly, there is an incentive for foreign and indigenous security forces to respond with lethal operations to strike back at the insurgents. "Many special operations units were originally formed specifically to conduct counterterror missions–that is, direct action. When deployed to Iraq and Afghanistan, it is only reasonable to expect them to do what they have been trained for" (Sepp 2010, 132).

A good example is the U.S. experience with the Phoenix Program in Vietnam. The Phoenix Program placed infrastructure neutralization (killed, captured, or rallied) quotas on the intelligence and operations coordinating centers and used the total number of infrastructure personnel neutralized to determine if the campaign were successful

(Tovo 2006). However, this approach confused measures of performance with measures of effectiveness.

The objective of the Phoenix Program was to limit the infrastructure's ability to support operations and exercise control over the population. Neutralization numbers did not measure whether the overall campaign was making progress towards these objectives. The second problem with the Phoenix Program quotas was that they caused dysfunctional organizational behavior. Driven to achieve neutralization quotas, police and military units often detained innocent civilians in imprecise cordon and sweep operations (Tovo 2006, 31). The overburdened legal system then took weeks or months to process detainees; the jails and holding areas provided the Viet Cong with an excellent environment for recruiting and indoctrinating previously apolitical civilians. The quota system bred corruption, as families paid bribes to secure the release of their relatives while others settled personal scores by identifying their personal enemies as members of the Viet Cong infrastructure (Tovo 2006, 31).

Similarly, foreign and indigenous security forces are also encouraged to develop and utilize their own irregular counterinsurgency forces, which are then used to locate and kill insurgents in their bases and safe areas for the purpose of achieving attrition. Of the numerous missions irregular forces perform, two are especially relevant to counterinsurgency: training and advising of local forces and conducting covert operations against insurgents and other high-value targets. The latter is an important mission in eliminating the most dangerous insurgents.

This is the case under both population- and enemy-centric counterinsurgency theories, although the scope and scale of the operations would be larger in enemy-centric

51

operations. Nevertheless, creating such forces before a sufficient policing capability can result in "death squads" or "secret police" activity, which is fundamentally counterproductive to population-centric counterinsurgency (Killcullen 2009, 62). As a result, irregular forces in developing countries are often misused for political ends.

Security Force Corruption

Practitioners conducting security force assistance often identify corruption as a major constraint on the development of indigenous counterinsurgency forces (Iraqi Federal Police Advisor Guide 2010; Killcullen 2009). Although the connection between corruption and effectiveness is intuitive (e.g., nepotism in promotion and theft of payroll degrades combat readiness), corrupt security forces also detract from the establishment or maintenance of the rule of law.

The security forces are the most visible agents of the government and are expected to protect the population from insurgents and criminals. This requires security forces to connect with the population through engagement throughout local communities. Security foster better relationships when their operations treat the population with respect and decency, while maintaining authority and providing adequate security. Importantly, the goal of the security forces is to create a mutually beneficial relationship with the population. Security forces protect and secure the population, who in turn provide information on insurgents and criminals. Security forces then convert the information into intelligence and actions to make arrests or prevent criminal acts, which further secure the population. Because insurgents and criminals retaliate against those who provide such information, security forces must also protect the families of these informants.

The population is less likely to trust corrupt security forces. Specifically, security forces neglect their duty to protect the population when they use their position for personal financial gain or accept bribes from insurgent groups, criminals, or political elites. This is especially true in states where the security forces were used by political leaders to coerce and brutalize the population. Security forces are hindered by their own history in these circumstances. Corruption hinders security forces from adhering to the rule of law and foster legitimate governance.

Arguably, the corrupt practices described above are obvious and security forces are likely to take active measures to reduce or eliminate them. Yet, this assumes an ethnocentric view of counterinsurgency operations, i.e., that the security forces are the arbiters of what constitutes corruption. However, security forces are at risk to neglect the possible ways that their conduct may be interpreted by the indigenous population as being corrupt. As discussed previously, security forces often ignore or contravene judges' orders. The population perceives these acts as arbitrary and disrespectful of the legal process. Yet from the perspective of security forces, it is merely an effort to correct substantive defects in the judicial process.

For example, security forces may free suspects because they are convinced that the evidence against them was obtained through coerced confessions elicited after beatings or torture. At other times, security forces order the continued detention of suspects when they are convinced that judicial release orders were influenced by nepotism, bribery, or intimidation (Stromseth et al. 2006, 323). These acts are well intentioned and in accordance with the substantive values associated with the rule of law. Nevertheless, they have the inevitable appearance of being arbitrary and capricious from the perspective of the indigenous population. Obviously, security forces do not intend this result.

Institutional Logic

Similar to structural mechanisms that explain people's choices as a direct function of their position in a material landscape, i.e., an exogenous obstacle course of physical constraints and resources, institutional mechanisms employ a logic-of-position where rational individuals confront an obstacle course comprised of man-made organizations, rules, or conventions. To separate institutionalist claims from structural causality, these constraints must be unintended legacies of past choices made amid structural ambiguity or unpredictability, not intentional solutions or adaptations to structural conditions (Parsons 2007). I describe below two institutional mechanisms affecting counterinsurgency security forces: (1) their civil-military tradition, and (2) their force rotation schedule.

Civil-military tradition

A state's civil-military tradition has a significant impact on its ability to conduct counterinsurgency operations or to advice and assist host nation security forces to do the same. Specifically, two major Western traditions, based on national culture, have been used to produce forces for executing security tasks in post-conflict settings (Orr 2004; Record 2007). One is an Anglo-American model that avoids domestic paramilitary police forces; the second is the continental model that embraces domestic paramilitary forces.

The Anglo-American model results in a force structure that emphasizes regular military forces over paramilitary and police forces. Consequently, states such as the U.S.

take these traditional military forces organized, equipped, and trained for combat, and utilize them for counterinsurgency. Yet, military security forces lack the ability to perform normal, non-threatening neighborhood law enforcement and public safety functions. Moreover, as discussed above, military forces are inherently poorer at using rectitude and discriminate force. Thus, the simple two-tiered (police-and-military) model to which the U.S. utilizes, in part because of their civil-military tradition, it inherently limiting.

The second major Western tradition is illustrated by counties with a tradition of national police organizations that possess paramilitary skills (Orr 2004; Record 2007). Under the continental model, security forces offer capacity that spans the gap between normal policing and military forces. They are specially equipped and trained for either large-formation operations as an adjunct to the military or for more dispersed and localized police functions. The Italian Carabinieri, the French Gendarmarie, and the Spanish Guardia Civil are examples (Gompert and Gordon 2008, 187-88). These organizations are composed of policemen but are capable of military-like actions in situations in which local police lack the training, firepower, and other specialized equipment to overcome heavy insurgent resistance.

Under this tradition, paramilitary police are able to function with regular police, with regular military forces, and on their own. In the Balkans in the 1990s, for example, the Carabinieri and military police units from other nations, operating under Carabinieri control, were able to diffuse difficult, riot situations with minimal use of force, backing up less well-armed local police (Gompert and Gordon 2008, 188). The paramilitary nature of these constabulary units provided them the option of quickly transitioning to the use of more force if the need arose.

Consequently, a state's civil-military tradition can significantly assist or hinder their ability to conduct counterinsurgency operation in accordance with the rule of law. Importantly, a state's civil-military tradition is an unintended legacies of its past choices (socio-political and legal, to name just a few) made during the state's formation or as a product of political evolution. These traditions are not an intentional solutions or adaptation to the requirements of counterinsurgency force management.

Force Rotation Schedule

Another institutional constraint derives from a state's decision to rotate counterinsurgency forces in to and out of the theatre of operation. Scholars have critiqued the U.S. military's ability to build effective local forces, citing the performance of police in Iraq and Afghanistan (Gompert and Gordon 2008, 231). This deficiency, in part, stems from the U.S. policy that rotated units and advisors yearly. Such rotations hinder continuity and personal relationships, which are vital in developing local counterpart forces (Nagl 2005). Quality of the indigenous security forces is more important than quantity. Because it takes time to train high-quality forces, especially in countries that have not had such forces, short troop rotations that fail to provide continuity of training that would inculcate rule of law principles into indigenous security forces. In this way, U.S. policy, created to address unrelated force generation and retention concerns, unintentionally hindered the military's ability to conduct counterinsurgency operations.

56

Ideational Logic

Ideational claims are a logic-of-interpretation that explains that individuals arrive at actions only through one interpretation of what is possible or desirable (Parsons 2007, 13). Ideational claims do so by asserting that persons have historically situated ways of interpreting things around them (Parsons 2007, 13). I describe below two ideational mechanisms that constrain security forces from adhering to the rule of law: (1) the preference to use conventional the security forces, and (2) the preference to conduct lethal operations. Both ideational mechanisms are counterintuitive and relate to how military commanders employ their security forces.

Conventional Security Forces

Intuitively, we should expect that states would deploy and then utilize security forces that best support the circumstances just described, since it is in a state's interest to properly construct and train forces to accomplish their mission. In fact, a popular critique of the U.S. military is that it is generally not well prepared to conduct post-conflict security and counterinsurgency, because its forces are trained and equipped principally to fight and win wars. Critics support this critique by positing that maintaining the peace in the aftermath of war requires a different forces, doctrine, training, and equipment than fighting the war itself (Nagl 2005). However, we know empirically that states often deploy conventionally trained forces with the capacity to deliver massive firepower to conduct counterinsurgency despite the obvious incompatibility (Nagl 2005).[10]

---

[10]It is arguable that another factor contributes to the use of conventional forces to conduct counterinsurgency. Namely, conventional forces are often the only forces available in a post-conflict environment, because they are already present in the theater of

Thus, the issue is not whether security forces are capable of using coercive power; rather, the issue is whether security forces will exercise rectitude and restraint in the exercise of that power. Yet, having deployed conventionally trained troops and large amounts of firepower, the counterinsurgency commander generally feels compelled to use them (Nagl 2005; Rid et al. 2010).[11] In other words, the counterinsurgent commander is induced by a historical and social construction to employ security forces contrary to espoused doctrine, simply because those forces are available for use.

Lethal Operations

Similarly, scholars have recognized that organizations favor policies that will increase the importance of the organization, seek to obtain and protect capabilities that they view as essential to their essence, and demonstrate comparative indifference to functions not viewed as essential (Allison and Halperin 1972). In other words, organizations develop an organizational culture. By virtue of long years of training and education, officers are inculcated with patterns of thinking that reflect this culture (Long 2006). Thus, military leaders are induced to favor the employment of forces and the conduct of operations in accordance to the military culture to which they are a part. However, for some these patterns are both incredibly useful in high-intensity conflict and incredibly inappropriate in counterinsurgency. Long provides several examples:

---

operations following the end of armed conflict. Nevertheless, it is conventional forces that find themselves tasked to conduct counterinsurgency operations.

[11]Many special operations units were originally formed specifically to conduct counterterror missions. Rid acknowledges that when these units were deployed to Iraq and Afghanistan, it is only reasonable to expect them to do what they have been trained for (Rid et al. 2010, 132).

One is the search for decisive battle. Another is the drive to maximize use of available firepower. The understandable desire to protect and provide comfort to their units encourages officers to (1) adopt force protection measures that limit effectiveness and (2) create large, comfortable bases away from the population. These patterns are so deeply inculcated that officers seldom recognize them, much less correct them. (Long 2006, 26-27)

Thus, the counterinsurgent commander induced to employ security forces contrary to espoused doctrine, because of the military culture to which he belongs.

Psychological Logic

Psychological claims assert that people perceive the world around them through hard-wired instincts, affective commitments, and/or cognitive shortcuts (Parsons 2007, 13). With the exception of rare variants that are just about hard-wired preferences of rational actors, they always imply irrationality (Parsons 2007, 13). I describe below a psychological factor that explains why security forces deviate from the rule of law when conducting counterinsurgency. Namely, counterinsurgent forces that are violently attacked reciprocate with indiscriminate violence.

As expressed in the literature reviewed above, insurgent and counterinsurgent forces struggle for the control of the populace through their use of coercive power and their ability to foster legitimacy. These factors are not mutually exclusive and are often utilized by both sides of the conflict to various degrees simultaneously. The population's support for the government and, by extension counterinsurgency forces, is conditional. Force has the potential to weaken and strengthen both the insurgency and the perception of incumbent regime's legitimacy. Thus, the literature strongly suggests that counterinsurgency is likely to succeed when security forces use coercive force legitimately, practice rectitude, and adhere to principles that foster legitimate governance, i.e., principles contributing to the rule of law.

Thus, we would expect to see security forces acting in accordance with the rule of law; specifically, security forces should use force only discriminately, even when attacked by insurgents. Nevertheless, security forces often do the opposite. O'Neil offers the examples of the Peruvian and Sri Lankan governments, whose armed forces were responsible for large-scale violence against civilians in the mid-1980s when responding to terrorist attacks (2005, 160). Similarly, he provides the example of Northern Ireland during 1960s. Here, the British initially responded with indiscriminate force, but modified their approach.

> [The] British initially reacted to IRA violence by relying on military units and harsh policies such as internment without trial, which was perceived as unjust, indiscriminate, and abusive. When this backfired, contributing instead to increased Catholic support for the IRA, the British rethought their policy, opting for more judicious treatment of suspects, enhanced discipline for military units, and a gradual turnover of the antiterrorist mission to police forces that received support (especially intelligence) from the military. (O'Neil 2005, 175)

Contrast these operations with those of security forces conducting counterinsurgency in accordance with the enemy-centric theory. According to that approach, violence is effective and efficient. Yet, this approach is fundamentally at odds with population-centric theory. Moreover, the aforementioned psychological claim provokes security forces to use indiscriminate violence even through theory and doctrine requires restraint.

The result of these psychological mechanisms is an escalating and indiscriminate use of military firepower. The expected derivative consequence of this escalation is often an increase in the security forces alienation from the population. Consequently, counterinsurgency dominated by conventional forces and lethal operations fails to adhere to rule of law principles as prescribed by population-centric counterinsurgency theory.

Conclusion

In this chapter I utilize the counterinsurgency and rule of law literature described in chapter 2 to explain why U.S. Army rule of law doctrine contained in FM 3-07 and the *Rule of Law Handbook* is more suitable for counterinsurgency than the current rule of law doctrine contained in FM 3-24. As discussed above, the key aspects of the rule of law posited by FM 3-24 unnecessarily incorporate too much substantive rule of law theory. This reliance on substantive principles is contrary to other U.S. Army doctrine regarding the rule of law and inconsistent with the themes of counterinsurgency appearing throughout FM 3-24. Thus, I conclude that the rule of law framework found in other U.S. Army doctrine is more suitable for counterinsurgency and propose its use for the analysis conducted in the remaining sections of this chapter.

Building upon the counterinsurgency theory explained in chapter 2, I describe why security forces that follow the rule of law are more likely to defeat an armed insurgency in the second section of this chapter. This is true for two reasons. First, their coercive power is more credible when used with rectitude and used discriminately. Second, operations conducted under the rule of law foster perceptions of legitimacy. This is accomplished under the hearts and mind approach through our expanded notion of security, under the rational actor approach through the employment of the proper incentives and sanctions, and under the transformational approach through the creation of alternative grievance mechanisms.

Lastly, I identify and describe several hidden or counterintuitive factors that influence counterinsurgency forces from following the rule of law. Specifically I use structural, institutional, ideational, and psychological causal logics to show on factors such as force composition, rotation patterns, corruption, civil-military traditions, military culture, and irrational psychological motivations influence operations.

In chapter 5, I draw from this analysis and make specific conclusions and recommendations regarding U.S. Army doctrine. I will also offer suggestions for future study.

CHAPTER 5

CONCLUSIONS AND RECOMMENDATIONS

Conclusions

I examined in the preceding chapters the insurgency and rule of law theories within the context of security forces conducting counterinsurgency operations. By examining and analyzing the relevant portions of these theories, I provide the conclusions listed below.

First, current U.S. Army doctrine regarding the rule of law contained in FM 3-24 conflicts with other U.S. Army rule of law doctrine, is internally inconsistent, and is unsuitable for use in counterinsurgency. I make this conclusion by illustrating how other U.S. Army rule of law doctrine, contained in FM 3-07 and the *Rule of Law Handbook*, more wisely incorporates competing rule of law theories and formulates a rule of law framework appropriate for counterinsurgency operations. This framework balances competing rule of law theories and takes a conservative approach regarding the inclusion of controversial and unnecessary substantive rule of law principles.

Second, security forces conducting counterinsurgency operations are more likely to defeat an armed insurgency if their operations are conducted in accordance with the rule of law framework described in FM 3-07 and the *Rule of Law Handbook*. I make this conclusion by describing how two critical aspects of population-centric counterinsurgency theory connect to the rule of law.

Specifically, security forces influence the population through two instruments – credible coercive power and popular perceptions of legitimacy. Thus, I determined that their coercive power is more credible when used with rectitude and used discriminately.

These two factors are also tenets of the rule of law's principle that the state is bound to protect its populace in person and property. Additionally, by addressing the three approaches to population-centric counterinsurgency I found that operations conducted under the rule of law foster perceptions of legitimacy. This is accomplished under the hearts and mind approach through our expanded notion of security, under the rational actor approach through the employment of the proper incentives and sanctions, and under the transformational approach through the creation of alternative grievance mechanisms.

Lastly, I identified and described several hidden or counterintuitive factors that influence counterinsurgency forces from following the rule of law. Specifically I used structural, institutional, ideational, and psychological causal logics to describe how several factors such as force composition, rotation patterns, corruption, civil-military traditions, military culture, and irrational psychological motivations influence operations.

Recommendations

1. Based on my conclusion regarding the rule of law framework contained in U.S. Army doctrine, I recommend that FM 3-24 be revised. Specifically, I recommend that the aspect of the rule of law contained in FM 3-24 be removed and that the rule of law framework contained in FM 3-07 and the *Rule of Law Handbook* be inserted.

2. Based on my conclusion that security forces conducting counterinsurgency operations are more likely to defeat an armed insurgency if their operations are conducted in accordance with the rule of law, I recommend that U.S. Army rule of law doctrine emphasize the importance of security forces conducting operations in this manner. Consideration should be given to revising the *Rule of Law Handbook* to acknowledge the importance that the rule of law plays to security forces conducting counterinsurgency.

This would constitute a much broader consideration of the rule of law to military practitioners, and would emphasize the importance of conducting security forces assistance to host nation security forces so that they conduct operations in this manner.

3. Based on my identification and examination of hidden and counterintuitive causal factors that assist or hinder security forces to conducting counterinsurgency operations under the rule of law, I recommend commanders consider these complex causal influences during the planning and conduct of operations in order to better conduct counterinsurgency operations. I also recommend that commanders encourage their staffs to utilize these causal logics in their planning and analysis.

4. I recommend that further research be conducted to examine whether there is empirical evidence that supports or contradicts my theoretical conclusion that security forces conduct counterinsurgency more effectively when adhering to the rule of law.

REFERENCE LIST

Allison, Graham T., and Morton H. Halperin. 1972. Bureaucratic politics: A paradigm and some policy implications. *World Politics*, vol. 24, *Supplement: Theory and Policy in International Relations* (Spring): 40-79

Arendt, Hannah. 1963. *On revolution*. New York: Viking

Cohen, Eliot A., John Horvath, and John Nagl. 2006. Principles, imperatives, and paradoxes of counterinsurgency. *Military Review* (March-April): 49-53.

Fallon, Richard H. 1997. The rule of law as a concept in international discourse. *Columbia Law Review*, 97: 7-8.

Galula, David. 1964. *Counterinsurgency warfare: Theory and practice*. New York: Praeger.

Gompert, David C., and John Gordon. 2008. *War by other means: Building complete and balanced capabilities for counterinsurgency*. Santa Monica, CA: RAND.

Joes, Anthony James. 2006. *Resisting rebellion: The history and politics of counterinsurgency*. Lexington, KY: University of Kentucky.

Kilcullen, David. 2009. *The accidental guerrilla: Fighting small wars in the midst of a big one*. Oxford: Oxford University Press.

Kitson, Frank. 1991. *Low intensity operations: Subversion, insurgency and peacekeeping*. London: Faber and Faber.

Long, Austin G. 2006. *On "other war": Lessons from five decades of RAND counterinsurgency research*. Santa Monica, CA: RAND, National Defense Research Institute.

Mack, Andrew J.R. 1975. Why big nations lose small wars: The politics of asymmetric conflict. *World Politics* 27, no. 2: 175-200.

McCuen, John J. 1966. *The art of counter-revolutionary war: The strategy of counter-insurgency*. Harrisburg, PA: Stackpole.

Merom, Gil. 2003. *How democracies lose small wars: State, society, and the failures of France in Algeria, Israel in Lebanon, and the United States in Vietnam*. Cambridge, UK: Cambridge University Press.

Murray, Williamson, and David H. Huntoon. 2006. *Strategic challenges for counterinsurgency and the global war on terrorism*. Carlisle, PA: Strategic Studies Institute, U.S. Army War College.

66

Nagl, John A. 2005. *Learning to eat soup with a knife: Counterinsurgency lessons from Malaya and Vietnam.* Chicago: University of Chicago.

Nevin, John A. 2003. Retaliating against terrorists. *Behavior and Social Issues* 12: 109-128.

O'Neill, Bard E. 2005. *Insurgency and terrorism: From revolution to Apocalypse.* Washington, DC: Potomac.

Orr, Robert C. 2004. *Winning the peace: An American strategy for post-conflict reconstruction.* Washington, DC: CSIS.

Parsons, Craig. 2007. *How to map arguments in political science.* Oxford: Oxford University Press.

Posner, Richard A. 2003. *Law, pragmatism, and democracy.* Cambridge: Harvard University Press.

Record, Jeffrey. 2007. *Beating Goliath: Why insurgencies win.* Washington, DC: Potomac.

Rid, Thomas, and Thomas A. Keaney. 2010. *Understanding counterinsurgency: Doctrine, operations and challenges.* London: Routledge.

Scalia, Antonin. 1989. The rule of law as a law of rules. *University of Chicago Law Review*, 56: 1175.

Sepp, Kalev I. 2010. Special forces. In *Understanding counterinsurgency: Doctrine, operations and challenges*, edited by Thomas Rid and Thomas A. Keaney, 128-140. London: Routledge.

Stromseth, Jane E., David Wippman, and Rosa Brooks. 2006. *Can might make rights?: Building the rule of law after military interventions.* Cambridge: Cambridge University Press.

Summers, Robert S. 1993. A formal theory of the rule of law. *Ratio Juris* 6: 127-135.

Thompson, Robert. 1966. *Defeating communist insurgency: The lessons of Malaya and Vietnam.* New York: F.A. Praeger.

Tovo, Ken, 2006. From the ashes of the Phoenix: Lessons for contemporary counterinsurgency operations. In *Strategic Challenges for Counterinsurgency and the Global War on Terrorism*, edited by Williamson Murray and David H. Huntoon, 21-32. Carlisle, PA: Strategic Studies Institute, U.S. Army War College.

Ucko, David H. 2009. *The new counterinsurgency era: Transforming the U.S. military for modern wars.* Washington, DC: Georgetown University Press.

U.S. Army. Headquarters Department of the Army. 2006. FM 3-24, *Counterinsurgency*. Washington, DC: USA HQDA, December.

———. 2008. FM 3-07, *Stability operations*. Washington, DC: USA HQDA, October.

U.S. Army. The Judge Advocate General's Legal Center and School, Center for Law and Military Operations. 2011. *Rule of law handbook: A practitioner's guide for judge advocates*. Charlottesville, VA: USA TJAGLCS.

Waldron, Jeremy. 2002. One law for all? The logic of cultural accommodation, *Washington and Lee Law Review*, 59: 3.